Flutes

Music Makers

THE CHILD'S WORLD®, INC.

Flutes

Pamela K. Harris

THE CHILD'S WORLD®, INC.

Library of Congress Cataloging-in-Publication Data
Harris, Pamela K., 1962–
Flutes / by Pamela K. Harris.
p. cm.
Includes index.
Summary: Simple text briefly describes flutes,
how certain kinds differ, and how they are played.
ISBN 1-56766-678-7 (library reinforced)
1. Flute—Juvenile literature. [1. Flute.] I. Title.
ML935 .H37 2000
788.3'19—dc21   99-058445

Credits

Translation: Neil Carruthers,
University of Canterbury, Christchurch, New Zealand
Graphic design: Brad Clemmons

Photo Credits

© www.comstock.com: 13, 20
© EyeWire: 7
© Hulton Getty/Liaison Agency: 19
© PhotoDisc: 15, 16, 23
© Stone/Michael Banks: cover, 3, back cover;
   Howard Kingsnorth: 9; Barbara Haynor: 10

Table of Contents

The Flute

Parades are fun to watch. There are floats and funny clowns. All kinds of bands march through the streets, too. As they pass by, you can see many shiny instruments. Did you notice the long silver-colored instruments in the bands? Those are flutes.

Flutes belong to a group of instruments called **woodwinds**. Clarinets and saxophones are woodwinds, too. To play a woodwind, you blow air into it.

Can you find the flutes in this parade? →

The Flute's Body

The body of a flute is a long tube. To play it, you hold the flute close to your lips. Then you blow air gently over the **mouthpiece**. The air **vibrates** inside the flute. The vibrating air makes the sound you hear.

Getting the right amount of air over the ➜ mouthpiece takes lots of practice.

What Are Flutes Made From?

Long ago, people discovered that they could blow into almost anything shaped like a tube and make a sound. People began to make flutes out of things such as shells and bones. Today flutes are made from wood, metal, plastic, and even glass!

← This man from India is playing a bamboo flute.

The Diameter of a Flute

The **diameter**, or width, of the flute's body changes the flute's sound. You can try this to see how it works. Blow into a wide bottle. Blow into a skinny bottle. Do they sound the same?

Flutes can make very low and very high sounds. ➡

The Holes of a Flute

Most flutes have holes in them. The holes can be close together or far apart. Flute players cover the holes with their fingers to make different sounds, or **notes**. When the player covers lots of holes, the flute makes low notes. When the player leaves lots of holes open, the flute makes high notes.

Most flutes have eight holes. Why do you think a flute would have eight holes? Some flutes have more holes, and some flutes have fewer. The *shakuhachi* (shah-koo-HAH-chee) flute from Japan has four holes. The *kena* (KAY-nah) flute from South America has five holes.

How many holes do you see on these *kena* flutes? ➡

Different Kinds of Flutes

Some flutes can make only one note. Others make many different sounds. A short flute makes high notes. A long flute makes low notes. A **pan flute** is a special type of flute. It is made by putting lots of smaller flutes together. Each of the smaller flutes plays a different note.

Another type of flute is called a **recorder**. Recorders are very old instruments that come from Asia. Long ago, recorders were made from wood. Today most recorders are made from plastic.

← A *pan flute* like this one is made of many different flutes.

More than 500 years ago, recorders were played for royalty. Kings and queens had servants who specialized in music and poetry. The servants sang and played recorders as the king and queen listened!

If you cover all the holes on a recorder, the note is very low. Take off one finger at a time. The note gets higher. This is how you make different notes.

This boy is practicing the *recorder* in school. ➡

Flutes that are played in orchestras and bands have more than eight holes. They also have **keys** with pads that cover the holes. You can play many notes on this type of flute.

← This flute's keys look like silver buttons.

Flutes Are Everywhere

Flutes can be found all over the world. People play flutes for ceremonies, for dancing, or just for fun. You can make your own flute. What kind of music would you like to play?

Other Woodwind Instruments

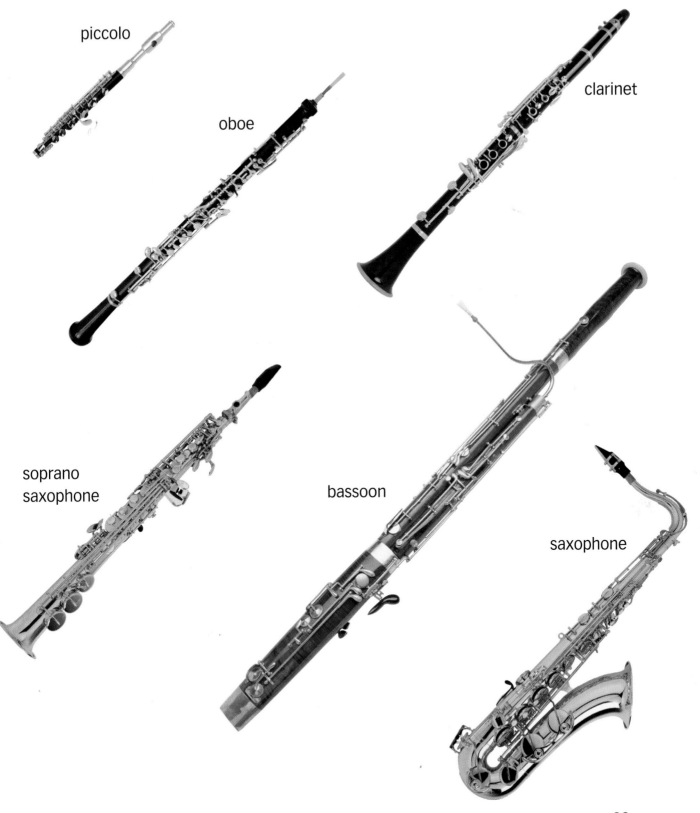

piccolo

oboe

clarinet

soprano
saxophone

bassoon

saxophone

Glossary

diameter (dy-AM-eh-ter)
A flute's diameter is its width. Wide diameters make low notes, and narrow diameters make high ones.

keys (KEEZ)
The keys of a flute are the buttons that help cover the flute's holes. Some flutes have many keys.

mouthpiece (MOWTH-peese)
The mouthpiece of a flute is where you put your mouth to play it. Blowing air over the mouthpiece creates sounds.

notes (NOHTS)
A note is a musical sound. By pressing different keys on a flute, a player can make different notes.

pan flute (PAN FLOOT)
A pan flute is an instrument made by putting smaller flutes of different sizes together.

recorder (ree-KOR-der)
A recorder is a type of flute that has eight holes. Recorders are very old instruments.

vibrates (VY-brayts)
When something vibrates, it moves back and forth. When air vibrates inside of a flute, it makes a sound.

woodwinds (WOOD-windz)
Woodwinds are tube-shaped instruments that are played by blowing air into a mouthpiece. Flutes are woodwinds.

Index